THE
NILE

THE NILE

BY
AARON W.
PERCEFULL

FRANKLIN WATTS
New York | London | Toronto | Sydney
1984 | A FIRST BOOK

Map by Vantage Art, Inc.

Cover photograph courtesy of
The Image Bank

Photographs courtesy of:
United Nations: pp. 4, 57;
The Bettmann Archive: pp. 11, 17, 20;
Ewing Galloway: pp. 12, 51, 54;
New York Public Library Picture Collection:
pp. 27, 31, 35, 36, 46.

Library of Congress Cataloging in Publication Data

Percefull, Aaron W.
The Nile.

(A First book)
Includes index.
Summary: Traces the modern history of the Nile River,
emphasizing the efforts of nineteenth-century explorers
to discover the river's source and twentieth-century
projects to exploit its resources.
1. Nile Valley—Juvenile literature. [1. Nile River.
2. Rivers] I. Title.
DT115.P43 1984   962   84-5167
ISBN 0-531-04828-4

CONTENTS

FOR
DORETTA AND TOOTS

thanks for the memories

THE
NILE

CHAPTER ONE

THE TWO NILES

The Nile. The very name of the great river covers seven thousand years of recorded human history. For it was here, in the valley of the Nile, that the history of civilization began. It was here that the ancient Egyptians built their great culture that for many years had no parallel. But here, in this same valley, that great culture finally died. All evidence of it lay buried, in the tombs and monuments along the Nile, for centuries. It was only rediscovered in modern times—after the American and French Revolutions.

Even more obscure and unknown was the river itself. Not even the ancients knew its source. It yielded its secrets only recently, as European and American explorers penetrated into the heart of Africa. The few brave men and women who went in search of the Nile had different reasons for their quests. Some came to put an end to slave trade; others were spurred on by religious zeal—to make the "heathen" Africans Christian. Still others came for fortunes in ivory and gold. But the best-remembered explorers came mainly for adventure. The Nile was a vast mystery and these discoverers would explain that mystery to all the world.

Today the Nile is a mystery no longer. Its sources are well known, and it has been thoroughly mapped along its entire 4,200-mile (6,720-km) length. The main tributary, known as the White Nile, begins at Lake Victoria in central Africa. Lake Victoria straddles the equator; it is the second largest lake in the world. It is 3,716 feet (1,115 m) above sea level. The lake is surrounded by the countries of Tanzania in the south, Uganda in the west and north, and Kenya in the northeast. Steamers run regularly from the southern port of Mwanza to Uganda and Kenya. African tribes once maintained small kingdoms on these shores. The modern state of Uganda was created from one such kingdom, and its capital, Kampala, is built on the site of the old capital.

The Nile begins its journey north at Jinja, on the north shore of Lake Victoria. Once there was a great rapids at that point, called Ripon Falls, but it has been submerged by a hydroelectric dam. The Nile then enters Lake Kioga before traveling on toward Lake Albert (also known today as Lake Mobutu). This part of the river is called the Victoria Nile. It passes over the Karuma and Murchison Falls, dropping a total of 1,700 feet (510 m) between Lakes Victoria and Albert. At Karuma Falls the water rushes in a great white foam past green islands. There is, today, an electric power station on the banks.

The Nile then flows into and out of Lake Albert. It receives waters from this lake and also from Lake Edward (also known as Lake Idi Amin). From Lake Albert to the Sudanese border, the river is referred to as the Albert Nile. Once in the Sudan it plunges over the Fola Rapids; now its name is Bahr el-Jebel (literally, Mountain Sea). It drops another 600 feet (180 m) to the town of Juba, capital of the southern Sudan. Here the river is still 1,483 feet (445 m) above sea level. It still has nearly 3,000 miles (4,800 km) to travel before reaching the Mediterranean Sea.

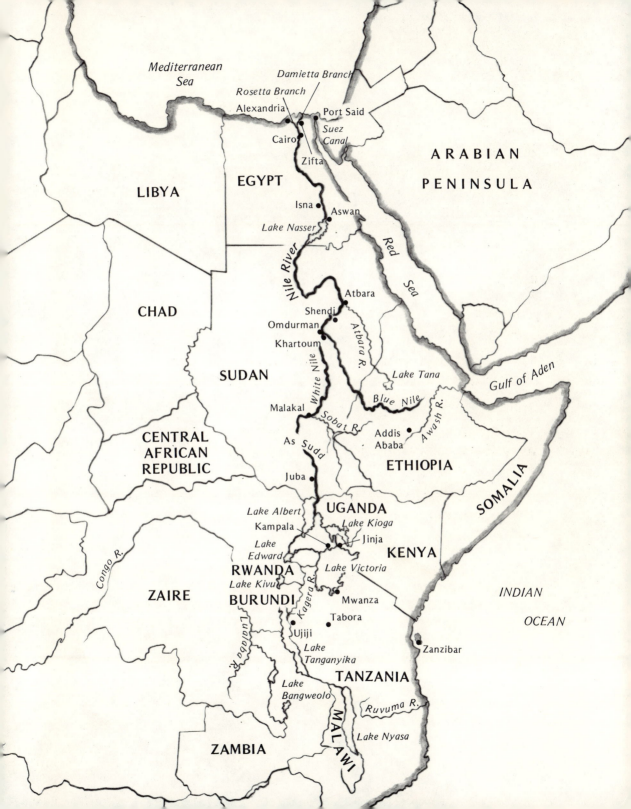

But the river then enters the great swamp known as the Sudd. Hundreds of square miles of papyrus reeds and water hyacinth spread on either side of the sluggish channel. The channel itself is at times only 40 to 50 yards (36.6 to 45.7 m) wide. The river finally leaves the swamp with a sudden turn east. Here it picks up the flow of the Sobat River, which comes from the Ethiopian Highlands. The river, now known as the White Nile, turns north toward Malakal. From Malakal to Khartoum, a distance of 500 miles (800 km), the river has no more tributaries. At Khartoum (the name means "elephant's trunk"), the White Nile is joined by the Blue Nile, its greatest tributary. At this point the united Nile is about 230 feet (69 m) above sea level.

The Blue Nile begins at Lake Tana in the Ethiopian Highlands, some 6,000 feet (1,800 m) above sea level. About 20 miles (32 km) downstream from Lake Tana the river goes over the Tisisat Falls, dropping 150 feet (45 m) to the gorge below. The Blue Nile then cuts a great gorge through the Ethiopian Plateau. At places the gorge is a mile (1.6 km) deep and 15 miles (24 km) wide. No one has ever traveled by boat or on foot down the length of the gorge. It is simply too dangerous a journey. The river travels 470 miles (752 km) from Lake Tana to the Sudanese border. It drops from 6,000 to 1,500 feet (1,800 m to 450 m) above sea level. Crocodiles and hippopotamuses live in its waters.

The mountains of Ethiopia turn into the plains of the Sudan and then all becomes desert. The Blue Nile broadens as it flows through the ancient kingdom of Sennar, finally joining the White Nile at Khartoum.

Tisisat Falls at
Lake Tana, Ethiopia,
the source of the
Blue Nile

The two rivers are very different in nature. The White Nile has traveled 2,000 miles (3,200 km) and dropped 2,000 feet (600 m) from Lake Victoria to Khartoum. In a much shorter distance the Blue Nile drops nearly 5,000 feet (1,500 m). When the two rivers merge, the Blue Nile has much more force. It is the water in the Blue Nile that causes the yearly Nile flood. In fact, the Blue Nile provides about 85 percent of the total volume of the river. For six months of the year the Blue Nile rushes out of Ethiopia almost like a tidal wave. June is the peak of this onslaught at Khartoum. The rush of water is so great that the White Nile is actually halted in its flow by the Blue. But by January the rush has ended.

From Khartoum the river travels another 1,750 miles (2,800 km) to the Mediterranean. It receives one more tributary, the Atbara, then no others. Now it flows through the Sahara Desert. There is no rain and no water—except for the mighty Nile itself. But it is here, about 180 miles (288 km) north of Khartoum, that the first signs of the ancient Egyptian civilization are seen. Near Shendi some two hundred ruined pyramids stand in the desert.

Now the Nile seems to stop, for it has reached the great reservoir behind the Aswan High Dam. This is Lake Nasser, in which many of the monuments of the ancient land of Nubia are now buried. Only fourteen of these monuments were saved, carefully moved to higher ground or to museums. The Nile also once had six gentle waterfalls, or cataracts, betwen Atbara and Aswan. They would normally disappear every year when the Nile flooded. Now two of them, the second and third, are submerged forever under Lake Nasser.

Below Aswan the wildness of Egypt ends. Both the crocodile and the hippopotamus have disappeared from the river here. There are birds, of course, but they are tamer than those upstream. And there are still, occasionally, the water buffalo, used to run the water wheels. And the great monuments of ancient Egypt are still here: Kom Ombo and Edfu, Karnak and Luxor, Dendera and Abydos. The Nile, now confined to a single channel, once spread out to form a fertile mouth, or delta. Long ago the Nile had seven mouths. Today the channel merely splits in two: the Rosetta branch and the Damietta branch. At the mouths of these two branches the great river finally enters the Mediterranean Sea.

CHAPTER
TWO

THE NILE
AND
ANCIENT EGYPT

Egypt was the home of the first great civilization. An extraordinary culture formed in that land four thousand years before Christ was born. It lasted for over two thousand five hundred years. Few cultures in all of human history have lasted so long and few have accomplished so much.

The great river Nile sits at the heart of all Egyptian achievement. Without the Nile there would have been no Egypt. The Nile is like a very long oasis. The valley it forms is green and life-giving. Outside this valley there is nothing but desert. The desert acts as a natural barrier and keeps intruders out. It kept the ancient Egyptians safe from attack. Thus they could live in peace along the banks of the Nile.

The ancient Egyptian civilization grew and flourished along the Nile between Aswan and the sea. This 750-mile (1200-km) stretch of the Nile is divided into two sections. For the last hundred miles the river fans out to form a delta. Many tributaries flow over the marshy land. This part of the Nile is known as Lower Egypt, or simply the Delta. South of the Delta the land is more arid. There the Nile runs between high, forbidding cliffs. This area is known as Upper Egypt.

Every year the Nile would rise above its banks and flood the surrounding land. This yearly flooding is what makes the Nile valley so fertile. The flooding begins with huge rainfalls in Ethiopia. The water from these torrential rains rushes north down the course of the Nile to the sea. As this huge amount of water moves north, it spreads itself over much of Egypt. This yearly flood provides Egypt with a sort of automatic irrigation. The flooding continues today, but it is controlled by dams.

But the flooding of the Nile is not entirely predictable. The ancient Egyptians knew there would always be a flood, but they never knew how big it would be. If the flood was too high, whole towns could be lost under the rising waters. If the flood was too low, much needed land was left dry and barren. From the beginning the ancient Egyptians tried to understand the Nile floods and how they could control them.

The great Egyptian civilization began when the people first learned how best to use the flooding. They had to plan carefully. First they watched the behavior of the river. They noticed the river had three "seasons." The first of these was called "Flooding," which started in June and ran through September. No planting could be done while the waters of the Nile rose. During this season the Egyptian people did whatever work their leader, the pharaoh, demanded. Often this meant hauling stones to build a tomb or temple for the pharaoh.

The second season was called "Planting." As the flood waters began to recede, the people would trap these waters as best they could to irrigate the land. Then the planting and tilling would take place. The third season was called "Drought." By this time the crops were fully grown and could be harvested. Grains were threshed, and stores of goods were put away for future use and for trading.

The early Egyptians developed clever ways of controlling the waters of the Nile. First they built dikes around their villages to keep them from being flooded. Then they made huge catch basins to trap the flood waters. A system of canals connected the catch basins to the fields.

The pharaohs needed to know how big the flood was going to be every year. They had gauges put on the river to measure the ebb and flow of the flood. These gauges, called nilometers, were first placed at Aswan and at what is now Cairo, and later pharaohs had them placed farther upstream. These nilometers gave the pharaoh early warning of how big a flood to expect.

The whole Egyptian economy depended on the Nile. It fed the people and was the primary source of Egypt's wealth. Egypt usually grew more than it could use, so much of this excess was exported, making Egypt rich.

The flooding of the Nile determined land values. Land that got flooded yearly was valued most highly—and taxed most highly by the pharaoh. Land that never saw the flood waters was valued little and was taxed accordingly.

Ancient Egypt was chiefly an agricultural nation. Though some gold was mined in Nubia, most of Egypt's wealth came from what it grew. One of Egypt's prime exports was truly a gift of the Nile. It was a reed which grew wild along the banks of the river, especially in the Delta. This tall reed was called papyrus. The Egyptians learned to make a sort of paper from this reed, and it was the best writing material available in the ancient world. Egypt was the sole source of papyrus. As a result, the Egyptian economy relied heavily on exports of papyrus paper for its well-being. Papyrus was used everywhere in the western world until the twelfth century, when rag paper was invented.

Papyrus was light in weight and could be rolled up. These

*Mosaic from the time
of Hadrian (76–138 A.D.)
showing life on the Nile*

—10—

*A replica of an ancient sailing vessel
in the Cairo Museum*

qualities made it clearly superior to heavy and cumbersome clay or wax tablets. It was used by scribes, accountants, and clerks throughout the Mediterranean world.

But papyrus had still other uses. The strong fibers of the plant could be made into excellent rope. The reeds could also be woven and bound together to form a variety of objects. Baskets and mats, sandals and sieves, even boats and fairly large ships were all made from papyrus. And Egypt exported much of what it made from the reed. Only grain exports brought in more wealth.

Not many trees grew in the Nile valley, so there was no wood for building. But there was a lot of mud. Early Egyptians learned how to make bricks from the mud for use in building.

Egyptians had to import olive oil because the olive tree did not grow well there. But they did have castor, flaxseed, and sesame oils to supplement their needs. Oil was very important to the Egyptians; they used it for many things. They cooked in it, used it in their lamps, and they also used it for cleansing themselves.

Ancient Egyptians also raised animals. Cattle and pigs thrived on the Delta. Goats could be found all over Upper and Lower Egypt. The marshes of the Nile housed water birds of all sorts, and some of these birds, like the ducks and geese, were trapped and fattened.

The Nile formed a natural path for getting from one place to another in Egypt. Goods could easily be transported up and down the river. Expensive overland travel was unnecessary. Nature also provided the Nile with a great advantage: the prevailing wind blows from the north, the river itself flows from the south, making travel on the river easy. A ship can drift with the currents downstream (from south to north). If it wants to go south again, it only has to put up its sails, catch the northerly wind, and the ship goes back upstream.

Naturally enough, the early Egyptians were sailors. An Egyptian pot dated 3200 B.C. shows a sailboat pictured on it. The Nile sailors mastered river travel and had different vessels for different purposes. There were little, sharp-nosed papyrus craft for getting through the narrow canals. Small boats, called punts, did everyday ferrying. Huge barges, often 200 feet (60 m) long, carried materials for the pharaoh's latest building project. There were even yachts and other grand pleasure vessels for the amusement of the wealthy.

The Nile unified not only a land but also a people. Controlling the power of the river was in the interest of all who lived along its course. Some sort of central government was necessary to gain such control over the river. Thus the First Dynasty came into being. Under its leaders, dikes were built and maintained, as were catch basins and irrigation canals. The work had to go on without stop, year after year, and because the work was so crucial, it involved the whole country. The central government of the First Dynasty had complete control over the people. Everyone was assigned duties and was expected to perform them: they were "drafted" to work for the government.

The pharaoh also used the Nile as a swift means of communication. He worked from a capital at Memphis (later moved to Thebes, farther south). Messengers traveled quickly up and down the river, keeping the pharaoh constantly in touch with his kingdom.

The Egyptian nation had little to fear from other nations. Its location neatly prevented attack from almost all sides. On both west and east are deserts. Caravans could cross the western wastes, but it was no route for an invading army. The Mediterranean Sea to the north was a possible invasion route, but it could be defended.

To the south was Nubia (today part of the Sudan). This area seldom supported a people powerful enough to defeat the Egyptians. Besides, travel down the Nile from Nubia was difficult because of the six cataracts on the Nile in Upper Egypt. Over the centuries the Egyptians extended their influence up the Nile. They moved from cataract to cataract and built forts along the way. Soon the entire length of the Nile from Khartoum to the Mediterranean was secure.

The ancient Egyptian felt, with good reason, that his life was secure. There was almost no threat of invasion. Internal upheavals were rare and not usually violent. It was a steady and quiet existence. But life was by no means easy for the common man. Peasants lived in small villages, in houses made of mud with high, slit windows. The buildings were crowded together, and there was little privacy. The towns were usually built between the fields by the Nile and the desert. Both men and women worked from dawn to dusk. Everyone had to help. Most men worked in the fields. Women, busy with household chores, also doubled as field hands. At harvest men, women, and children joined to gather the crops. A festival followed to celebrate the bounty of the harvest. During the season of Flood, the government had the men build dikes, canals, and, according to the pharaoh's whim, tombs, temples, and monuments.

Many peasants worked on the river itself, on barges, freighters, and ferries. There was much cross-river traffic. Ferries were always in demand. Most riverboats were built so that they could travel across very shallow water. They could be beached on the bank like a rowboat. Strangely enough, fishing for food was forbidden by royal decree. In many places certain fish were considered sacred. Any people who ate fish were thought to be "unclean." But the hungry peasants paid little attention to such laws. They fished often and were grateful for their catch.

But life was not without its pleasures. While the peasants' work was continual, they knew they would always have food and shelter. The most basic of needs were always met. Paintings from tombs suggest that peasants had an abundance of good cheer. These paintings often show children at play while their elders work, and the grown-ups are seen joking with one another as they go about their daily tasks.

It seemed at times that life along the Nile would continue

forever the same. And for two thousand years it did. But after the Twentieth Dynasty (about 1200 B.C.), the Egyptian civilization began a slow but steady decline. Egypt's political power grew less and less, and its neighbors grew stronger and stronger. There was much internal trouble in Egypt: Upper and Lower Egypt split apart and reunited several times. Egypt was invaded by Libyans, Nubians, and Assyrians. All came to take Egypt's wealth—the wealth of the Nile.

In 332 B.C. Egypt came under Greek control when it was conquered by Alexander the Great. When he died, Egypt was given to one of his field commanders, Ptolemy. Ptolemy was the first Egyptian ruler who was not a native of Egypt. Ptolemy's descendants ruled Egypt for three hundred years. Though they were of Greek ancestry, they lived in Egypt as Egyptians. The last of the Ptolemys was Cleopatra. She tried to unite Egypt and the Roman Empire. In this way she hoped Egypt could remain mostly independent from Rome. But Cleopatra failed. The Roman ruler Augustus Caesar would not give in to Cleopatra and he made Egypt a province of Rome. Cleopatra killed herself rather than be taken captive by the Romans, and with her the last hope of an ancient and proud land died.

Augustus Caesar annexed Egypt to the Roman Empire in 30 B.C. But the Egyptian city of Alexandria remained a center of Greek influence. It was there in A.D. 45, and again in A.D. 62, that St. Mark came to preach a new religion—Christianity. An Egyptian Christian community grew and split from other branches of Christianity. These Coptic Christians, as they were known, did not speak or write in Greek or Latin. Instead they used a very late form of the language of the ancient Egyptians. It was written with Greek characters.

The Christians of Alexandria suffered persecution until the entire Roman Empire became Christian in 313. When the Empire split into eastern and western sections, Egypt naturally became part of the Eastern Empire ruled from Constantinople.

*The city of Alexandria was the center of Greek influence
in northern Africa for hundreds of years.*

But in 640 Egypt was conquered by invading Arab armies of the new religion of Islam. The Moslems (as followers of Islam are known) effectively ruled Egypt and the Nile valley for six hundred years. Saladin, the Moslem ruler from 1171 to 1193, had many enemies. He developed an elite corps of Turkish cavalry known as the Mamelukes to protect him. The Mamelukes became very powerful in their own right and took control of Egypt in 1250.

The Ottoman Turks conquered Egypt in 1517, but the Mamelukes remained in Egypt as agents of the Ottomans. The Mamelukes eventually regained much of their former power, and they went unchallenged until Napoleon arrived in 1798. From that point Egypt was occupied by a succession of foreign rulers and would not know independence until 1953.

CHAPTER THREE

THE FRENCH ON THE NILE

Under the Mamelukes there was no commerce along the Nile. Few people even risked travel on the river unless they were well escorted. The Bedouin tribesmen who roamed the desert robbing caravans were also a danger on the Nile. Boats that ran aground on Nile sandbars (and there were many) were promptly robbed by the Bedouins.

By the late eighteenth century about 2.5 million people lived in Egypt; three times as many had lived there during the time of the pharaohs. Only two cities of any size remained: Alexandria and Cairo. The once-great Alexandria now had fewer than ten thousand residents, and almost nothing was left of its four thousand palaces, temples, and monuments. At its peak Alexandria had rivaled Rome in splendor and power. By the 1790s it was in ruins.

Napoleon, with forty thousand troops, arrived at the mouth of the Nile during the summer of 1798. He believed Egypt was of strategic importance to France. From an Egyptian base, France could move against the Ottoman Empire to the north in Turkey.

*Napoleon leading his troops to victory over
the Mamelukes in the Battle of the Pyramids*

Also, Napoleon hoped to build a canal across the Suez peninsula so that ships traveling from the east would not have to go around the tip of Africa, which was under British control. Napoleon saw the canal as a means of political persuasion. Countries the French favored would be allowed to use the canal. Other nations—especially England—would be forced to use the longer and more costly route around the tip of Africa. Napoleon planned to use the canal to put an economic squeeze on England. At the same time he believed France might one day use its Egyptian base to launch a campaign against the British colony in India.

Napoleon's plan for taking Egypt was elegant and simple. He proposed to take the Rosetta mouth of the Nile. Then his armies would follow the Nile to Cairo and take the capital.

It was all over very quickly. Although the Mamelukes were the first to attack, they were totally unprepared for the highly organized French artillery. The French easily turned back the attack, exhausted though they were. Very few of the Mamelukes even got close to the French, and those who did were easily stopped with handguns. In just a few minutes some forty Mamelukes were dead or wounded.

By July 13 the Mamelukes had formed a large force a little farther up the Nile. There were four thousand of them ready for battle, but Napoleon did not wait for their attack. Instead he went to meet them. The Mamelukes charged Napoleon's troops three times. Each time they were easily repelled, and by the end of the day three hundred Mamelukes had died. Of the French only seventy were killed.

But Murad, the Mameluke chief, would not recognize defeat. The Mamelukes were brave and fierce—they were also five hundred years behind the times. Clearly, Murad's forces could not compete against the modern French fighting machine. Still Murad carried on, in pride and desperation, to fight a war he could not possibly win.

The two forces met again on July 21, only 20 miles (32 km) from Cairo. This decisive skirmish was later to be called the Battle of the Pyramids, although the actual battle occurred nowhere near the pyramids. They were nine miles (14.4 km) away, but Napoleon referred to them as he prepared his troops for combat. "Soldiers!" he said, pointing in the direction of the distant pyramids. "Go and think that, from the top of these monuments, forty centuries are watching you."

Murad tried to aid his infantry but could not. The French had him cut off. The Mameluke camp was surrounded. French troops prevented escape on three sides and the Nile was on the fourth. The Mamelukes in their pride refused defeat. Dozens of them threw themselves into the Nile rather than surrender. They preferred suicide to submission. The entire battle lasted only an hour.

Napoleon marched into Cairo as victor. But he was no hero to the native Egyptians, the fellaheen. This was the first real contact between the West and Egypt since the Romans had left, and that was over one thousand years before. The fellaheen were suspicious, so Napoleon tried to put them at ease. He made a speech while dressed in Egyptian costume. The speech was all about the rights of man. "When I'm in France, I'm a Christian," the great general said. "When I'm in Egypt, I'm a Mohammedan." There would be no attempt to convert the fellaheen. There would be no religious persecution.

Napoleon would educate Egypt whether Egypt wanted it or not. He was ably assisted by the scholars he had brought with him. They set up an Egyptian Institute whose mission was to study thoroughly all of ancient and modern Egypt. The Institute also made plans for certain improvements. Plans were made for a Suez canal. The Nile's annual flood was to be studied. Plants and animals were investigated. Maps were to be made. New crops would be tried (especially cotton). Hospitals were begun, and doctors confronted diseases they had never seen before.

The French settled in at Cairo, but Napoleon was restless. He knew Murad had fled up the Nile with troops and at any time the Mamelukes might come down the river and attack the French. Napoleon felt it was important to make the Nile secure: Murad and the remaining Mamelukes had to be pursued and destroyed. He sent a group of about five thousand soldiers up the Nile under the leadership of his right-hand man, General Desaix. Napoleon also sent along one of his scholars—a brilliant man named Vivant Denon. As Desaix's troops went up the Nile, Denon took careful notes on everything he saw. He recorded, in words and drawings, the many monuments and tombs of the Nile valley. His report was the first modern account of the ancient Egyptian culture.

General Desaix spent a little over a year on the Nile in pursuit of Murad. There were repeated skirmishes between the French and the Mamelukes. But finally, in October 1799, Murad surrendered and pledged his allegiance to France. The remaining Mamelukes were cut off in the deserts of Nubia, and the Nile was secure from the Mediterranean to Aswan.

But the French glory in Egypt did not last long. The British and the Turks had blockaded Alexandria. Napoleon was completely cut off from France, although some news did manage to get through. The political situation in France was chaotic, so Napoleon decided to attempt to return to Paris. He intended to "chase out that gang of lawyers . . . who are incapable of governing the Republic." His departure was kept very secret. He left Egypt as soon as it seemed his ship could get through the blockade. General Kléber was left in charge of Egypt.

Napoleon arrived at Paris in October 1799. A month later he was France's dictator. But the situation in Egypt got worse for Kléber over the next eighteen months. Finally, in March 1801, a mixed British and Turkish force conquered Alexandria. Cairo fell without a struggle, and the French agreed to leave. By the end of 1801 the French were gone; the English left soon thereafter. Egypt was once more in Turkish hands.

CHAPTER FOUR

EARLY EXPLORATION OF THE NILE

Today exploration is taken for granted. People travel to the moon. They stay in outer space for weeks at a time. People no longer explore the totally unknown. No one landed on the moon until unmanned spaceships landed there first. Those unmanned ships gave scientists much information that told what the first people could expect and how they should prepare themselves.

But until recently exploration was different. Men and women traveled into unknown and uncharted territory with nothing to guide them but courage and faith. Maps of Africa were scarce and incomplete. Often large sections of the continent were left blank because no one knew what was there.

Most of the Nile was a total mystery. The lower Nile was known well enough, but the rest was uncharted. No one knew where it came from or what course it took. Just a few daring men made their way into the wilderness of the upper Nile and its tributaries.

The first of the great African explorers were Richard Francis Burton and John Hanning Speke. Both had been members of the Indian Army. They met in Aden in 1855 where they joined on an expedition. Next Burton and Speke planned their grand adventure—to find the source of the Nile. By the end of 1856 Burton had received £1,000 from the British Foreign Office to pay for the expedition. He also had the backing of the Royal Geographical Society in London. The two men prepared for their journey on the island of Zanzibar, off the coast of eastern Africa.

A typical caravan into the interior of Africa at this time took much preparation. Enough supplies were needed for at least a year, maybe more, and these supplies had to be carried by native porters. Supplies included scientific instruments, medicines, and guns of all sorts. Malaria was well known to be a great danger, so the medicine chest included quinine. Morphine was included for extreme pain.

The explorers also had plenty of camp furniture. Besides their tents they had portable beds, tables, chairs, blankets, mattresses, air pillows, mosquito nets, knives, forks, and other utensils for cooking. They planned to feed themselves mostly off whatever wildlife they could shoot or trap. They insisted on certain luxuries. These "extras" included brandy, cigars, tea, coffee, salt, pepper, pickles, soap, spices, and, in the best British tradition, umbrellas.

On June 16, 1857, they left Zanzibar for the mainland. The caravan finally numbered 132 in all. As it marched, the group sang, chanted, shouted, and made whatever noise it could because it was thought that noise would scare any local tribes thinking of attacking the caravan. On the trip inland, both Burton and Speke were constantly ill. Often they were hungry to the point of starvation.

Finally, after five long months of marching, the group reached Kazeh. (Kazeh is now called Tabora and is part of Tanzania.) Here they found about twenty-five Arab traders. They bought some provisions and rested for a month. Burton, who spoke Arabic, found out what little he could about the land they were about to explore.

Burton and Speke set off from Kazeh in early December. On February 13, 1858, they reached the shores of Lake Tanganyika at Ujiji. They explored the lake, hoping it would prove to be the source of the Nile. Instead they found the Ruzizi River flowing *into* the lake *from* the north. The Ruzizi would have to flow *out* of the lake and *toward* the north for it to be a possible source of the Nile. Burton was, as he later wrote, "sick at heart" that the source of the great river had not been found. (Later still, Burton would mistakenly insist that the Ruzizi flowed *out* of Lake Tanganyika. He wanted very much to believe he had found the source of the Nile—so much that he distorted the facts.)

The two explorers made their way back to Kazeh. Here supplies had come up from the coast and were waiting for them. Burton decided to stay in Kazeh for a while to rest and compile his notes. But Speke was impatient to go on; he had heard Arab reports of a great lake to the north. On July 10, 1858, Speke set off without Burton in search of the lake. Burton agreed to this arrangement reluctantly.

In less than a month Speke stood on the shores of a huge inland sea. This was the great "Nyanza" he had heard of from the Arabs. He called the lake Victoria, in honor of the Queen of England. At the same time Speke had a flash of insight. Lake Victoria, he declared, was the single source of the Nile. He came to this belief purely on instinct. There was, at the time, not a single bit of scientific evidence for his claim.

Naturally, Burton disputed Speke's claim. But the two remained friends, at least on the surface. They returned to England and both men quickly made their findings public. Burton published a scientific report about Lake Tanganyika. The public took little notice of it. But Speke fired the public's imagination. He went directly to Sir Roderick Murchison, President of the Royal Geographical Society, and quickly convinced Murchison

*The Victoria Nile as it flows north
from its source, Lake Victoria*

that another expedition was needed right away. Speke wanted to find the northern outlet of his Lake Victoria. Such an outlet would, he believed, prove that Lake Victoria was the source of the Nile. Murchison agreed, and the Society quickly provided £2,500 for the new expedition. Burton was not asked to join. Instead he was replaced by another Indian Army officer, Captain James Augustus Grant.

Speke's plan for the expedition was to take the same route he had taken before to Lake Victoria. Then he intended to go up the west side of the lake until he found its outlet in the north. The land he intended to go through—today mostly Uganda—was totally unexplored at the time. In fact Uganda then was made up of three separate kingdoms: Bunyoro in the north, Buganda in the center, and Karagwe in the south. These three kingdoms were totally isolated from the outside world. Speke and Grant were to be the first Europeans to set foot in the region.

It took Speke and Grant a year to reach the interior. They entered the unknown area of Karagwe in November 1861. Grant soon came down with malaria. Then he developed a terrible sore on his leg which prevented him from walking. Both Speke and Grant rested in Karagwe under the care of the local chief, Rumanika. He told them they must stay in Karagwe until Mutesa, chief in Buganda, "sent" for them. Messengers were dispatched ahead to Mutesa. In due course the answer came: The explorers were "requested" at Mutesa's court.

But Speke went on alone. Grant's leg caused him such pain that he could not move. He stayed behind in Karagwe under Rumanika's protection. It took Speke six weeks to reach Mutesa. After much delay, Speke was allowed to meet the Bugandan king. Speke offered presents: rifles, guns, ammunition, a gold watch, a telescope, beads, cloth, and various eating utensils. In return Speke was given cattle, goats, fish, game, porcupines, and rats. To Mutesa all these animals were food and therefore valuable.

Speke spent three months with Mutesa. Finally Grant arrived. His leg was barely healed and he limped badly, but the two were eager to get on with their search. Mutesa made them stay in his court another six weeks. Finally, on July 7, 1862, Mutesa let them go.

The caravan marched north of Lake Victoria. In fact they had gotten a little off course, and a sharp turn south was needed to end up at the outlet of the lake. Speke and Grant held a conference. It was decided that Grant would continue north into Bunyoro, where he would prepare the way for the expedition to continue north into Egypt. Speke, however, was to go south in search of the source of the Nile. By this time Speke was in a great hurry. The closer he came to his goal, the faster he pursued it. So Speke and Grant agreed to split up. Speke took off south at the rapid rate of 20 miles (32 km) a day. By July 21, 1862, he stood on the banks of the Nile. He was about 40 miles (64 km) downstream from Lake Victoria. He marched upstream and on July 28 he reached his goal. There before him a great stream poured from Lake Victoria, forming a waterfall. He named the falls Ripon Falls "after the nobleman who presided over the Royal Geographical Society when my expedition was got up."

Speke was certain that he had found the source of the Nile. He rejoined Grant a month later in Bunyoro, where King Kamrasi treated them rudely. They heard reports in Bunyoro of another great lake west of Victoria. Could it be yet another source of the Nile? The two explorers were too exhausted to investigate it. It was November 1862 and they had been gone for two years. Almost all their supplies were used up, lost, or given away to local chieftains. Now they had to concern themselves with one thing—survival. The other great lake to the west would have to wait for another time.

Five more months passed before Speke and Grant finally entered Gondokoro. Gondokoro, in the Sudan, was the outermost civilized settlement on the Nile. The two explorers were greeted there by Samuel Baker, a sportsman and explorer, and Baker's wife, Florence, who shared all her husband's adventures. The Bakers had come up the Nile in search of Speke and Grant. After two years' absence many had assumed that Speke and

Grant were lost forever. But there they were, exhausted and ragged, full of tales and discoveries. Speke was sure, this time. He had *seen* the source of the Nile. There could be no doubt about it, or so he thought.

But doubt there was. When he returned to England, Speke found himself in the midst of controversy. Burton, his former companion, insisted that Speke left too many questions unanswered. He accused Speke of "faulty geography." How could Speke be sure that the great body of water he saw on this trip was the same one he had seen on the last trip? Maybe there was more than one lake. And how could he be sure that the water leaving this lake at Ripon Falls was indeed the Nile? Had he traveled all the way around the lake to look for other outlets? Had he followed the stream he found to see if it did, indeed, become the Nile?

Of course Speke had done none of these things. Burton was right. Speke had no "hard" evidence that he had found the source of the Nile. The British Association for the Advancement of Science arranged for Burton and Speke to meet in a public debate. Among those planning to attend was the already famous African missionary-doctor, David Livingstone. The meeting was arranged for September 16, 1863, at Bath, England.

The debate was never to occur. The day before the great event, Speke accidentally shot himself in the chest while out hunting partridges with a cousin, George Fuller. There were no eyewitnesses to the accident, but Fuller was at Speke's side moments afterwards. Rumors persisted that Speke had committed suicide rather than face Burton in debate. There is little evidence to support such notions. Burton, for his part, cried for hours when he heard the tragic news about his former friend and colleague. Many years later, when the truth about the Nile's source was finally known, a plaque was put at Ripon Falls which said: "Speke discovered this source of the Nile on the 28 July 1862." Today that plaque and the falls themselves are submerged. The reservoir created by a hydroelectric dam has hidden them from view forever.

*John Hanning Speke (right) with James Grant
during Speke's return trip to Africa to prove
his declaration that Lake Victoria was the one
and true source of the Nile*

CHAPTER
FIVE

LATER
EXPLORATION
OF
THE NILE

In 1863, when Speke and Grant emerged from the Sudan, the source of the Nile was still unknown. Samuel Baker and his wife, Florence, now went on their own search for the source. They had come up the Nile looking for Speke and Grant. When the four met, they compared notes about the river. They also spoke of the American Civil War, which had caused such a drastic rise in the price of cotton and cotton fabric. This sudden rise in the cost of cotton would help Egypt to develop as a major cotton-growing nation. Speke and Grant told the Bakers about the great lake to the west of Lake Victoria. Perhaps it was another source of the Nile. It was toward this lake, called Luta Nzige by the natives, that the Bakers now went.

The Bakers faced many difficulties. Both suffered badly from malaria. Often Mrs. Baker had to be carried on a stretcher. In early 1864 the Bakers reached the Bunyoro region. King Kamrasi's men escorted the Bakers into his presence. The king declared Baker to be "Speke's brother." He forced the pair to stay with him for over a month. Finally he allowed them to leave in mid-February.

For another month the Bakers trudged on. Often Mrs. Baker was delirious or unconscious from fever. Baker, too, suffered feverish fits. Finally, on March 14, 1864, the Bakers saw a great body of water. Supported by each other, they walked slowly down to the lake's edge. Solemnly they gave the lake a name. They called it Albert, in honor of Queen Victoria's husband, who had recently died.

The Bakers believed they had found yet another source of the Nile. In fact, the Nile flows through the northern end of Lake Albert. In crude native canoes the Bakers paddled north on the lake. After two weeks they reached the point where the Nile flows into the lake. They traveled east along the river for a short way and discovered a spectacular waterfall, only 20 feet (6 m) across, but 130 feet (39 m) high. The Bakers called it Murchison Falls, after the President of the Royal Geographical Society at the time.

For six months the Bakers were forced to remain in Bunyoro. Tribal wars between the Bunyoro and the Buganda kept the Bakers from traveling anywhere. But for once the Bakers had good luck. An Arab caravan came to Bunyoro with supplies for the Bakers. They joined the Arabs and headed north, toward Gondokoro. They entered that city in February 1865 and finally reached the Suez in October. They had been gone for two years and were presumed dead. The Bakers had been in Africa for five years altogether, and on their return to London the Queen quickly made Baker a knight. Sir Samuel and Lady Baker became the favorites of London society.

But the Bakers' discovery of Lake Albert did not clear up the mystery of the Nile's source. Which lake, if either, was the true source of the Nile: Victoria or Albert? Or might Lake Tanganyika be the source? Burton was suddenly no longer sure if the Ruzizi River flowed into or out of that lake. Perhaps the Ruzizi connected Lakes Tanganyika and Albert. That would mean Lake Victoria could not be the source because it lay north of Lake Tanganyika.

Many questions remained to be answered. Sir Roderick Murchison of the Royal Geographical Society proposed a solution: send Dr. David Livingstone to find the answers. Livingstone, though already fifty-two at the time, certainly seemed the man for the job. For twenty-two years he had been a medical missionary in Africa and no one knew Africa better. Livingstone was a man of absolute honor. Also, he was a man of science.

Livingstone agreed to return to Africa. In March 1866 he entered the mouth of the Ruvuma River and began seven years of travels. It is amazing that Livingstone lasted a fraction of that time. Near the beginning of his journey he lost most of his men and animals, as well as his medicines. But in a year's time he reached Lake Tanganyika. Seemingly without purpose or direction he wandered about central Africa. He went west to the Lualaba River, then south to Lake Bangweolo. (No Europeans had ever been to this region.) Working his way north again, he came to Ujiji on Lake Tanganyika in March 1869. He had been in Africa three years. He was nearly toothless and almost dead from malaria. The supplies he expected to find waiting for him in Ujiji had not arrived.

Somehow Livingstone made it back to the Lualaba River. He was convinced it was the same river as the Nile. While on his journey there, he witnessed a horrible and senseless slaughter of natives by Arab slave traders in Nyangwe. His account of this massacre would eventually reach all the literate world. It alone would do more to stop slave trading than any other written words.

Livingstone wandered back to Ujiji once more, in even worse shape than he had been two years earlier. He had been gone from civilization for five years. His search for the source of the Nile had failed. Many people in Europe and America presumed Livingstone was dead.

David Livingstone

*The historic meeting of Stanley and Livingstone
in Ujiji on November 10, 1871. "Dr. Livingstone,
I presume?" queried the reporter.*

But Livingstone was about to be found, and by a most amazing man. Henry Morton Stanley was a reporter for the *New York Herald.* He was on assignment to find Livingstone when he marched into Ujiji on November 10, 1871. Stanley walked boldly up to the pale and weary old Livingstone. He did not know if Livingstone would be glad to see him or not; the doctor was known to dislike publicity. "Dr. Livingstone, I presume?" he said in his now much-quoted phrase. "Yes," the doctor answered with a smile, lifting his cap.

As Livingstone's health improved, the two planned a trip up Lake Tanganyika. On that trip they proved that the Ruzizi River flowed into the lake, not out of it, which meant Lake Tanganyika could not be a source of the Nile.

Livingstone was still convinced that the Lualaba River, flowing out of Lake Bangweolo, was the Nile's source. With Stanley he went to Tabora, where he waited while Stanley went on to the coast. Stanley promised to send Livingstone porters and equipment for another expedition to the Lualaba. Then Stanley returned to England and reported finding Livingstone alive. He also told Livingstone's account of the massacre at Nyangwe.

By August 1872 Livingstone had received the porters and supplies Stanley had promised. He set off once again for the Lualaba. He was sure that a stream running into Lake Bangweolo would prove the source of the Nile. But Livingstone's time ran out, and he never really knew his error. He was found dead in his tent on the shores of Lake Bangweolo on May 1, 1873. He was kneeling in prayer when his heart stopped.

His servants, Susi and Chuma, carried his body all the way back to the coast. The trip took eleven months. It was an incredible act of devotion. His body was then taken back to England, where he is buried in Westminster Abbey.

When Stanley returned to London in May 1872, everyone was thrilled he had found Livingstone alive. But Stanley had many enemies, too. Some critics saw Stanley's feat as a journalistic stunt; others went so far as to call it a hoax. Still others, full of

English pride, were angry that an American had found Livingstone (and this even though Stanley was born Welsh and would later become a British citizen again).

But Stanley knew he could succeed where others had failed. He began to plan a new African journey in 1874. He had three goals. The first was to travel all the way around Lake Victoria in a boat. By doing this, Stanley would prove the lake was a single body of water. He would also prove that the stream leaving the lake at Ripon Falls was its only outlet. Second, Stanley planned to travel all around Lake Tanganyika in a boat. He wanted to see if this lake had any outlet flowing north. If not, then it could not be a source of the Nile. Third, Stanley planned to sail down the Lualaba River to see if it joined the Congo River or the Nile.

Money came easily for the expedition. Two newspapers, the *New York Herald* and the *London Daily Telegraph*, gave Stanley everything he needed in exchange for rights to his reports of the trip. The expedition set out from Zanzibar for the mainland in November 1874. It was the best-equipped and largest African expedition ever. It included 356 men and a boat, *Lady Alice*, which came apart in sections so it could be easily carried.

The group reached Lake Victoria in March 1875. *Lady Alice* was assembled, and Stanley began his trip around the lake. The voyage took fifty-seven days. Stanley returned to his starting point in May. Victoria was in fact one huge lake. The outlet at Ripon Falls was the only major outlet. The only major intake proved to be the Kagera River on the west. Speke, it seemed, had been right: Lake Victoria was, for all practical purposes, the source of the Nile.

But Stanley still had to prove Burton's theories about Lake Tanganyika wrong once and for all. Stanley first spent some months with King Mutesa and then with King Rumanika. Then he and his group pushed south. They reached Lake Tanganyika in June 1876. In less than two months Stanley had sailed around the lake in *Lady Alice*. He returned with convincing proof: The lake had no outlet that could possibly be a source of the Nile.

Then in August 1876 Stanley began his journey down the Lualaba. He had absolutely no idea where the river would take him. The trip was a series of disasters. The riverside tribes attacked frequently, most of the supplies were lost, and the caravan suffered from starvation and fever. But finally Stanley and his group found themselves at the mouth of the Congo River. Only 114 of the 356 who started the trip in Zanzibar had survived.

Stanley had been away for 999 days. His expedition proved to be the greatest of them all. He had answered all the big questions about Africa. Lake Tanganyika was not the source of the Nile. Instead, the Nile started at Lake Victoria and flowed north through Egypt to the Mediterranean. And the Lualaba River joined the Congo and flowed west to the Atlantic. Stanley returned to Zanzibar in 1877, one of the most celebrated men of his time. The great search for the source of the Nile was finished.

CHAPTER SIX

COLONIZING THE NILE VALLEY

As British exploration of the Nile was taking place, the Nile valley underwent some dramatic political changes. Ismail, grandson of Mohammed Ali, who founded the modern ruling dynasty, became the Khedive (or viceroy) of Egypt in 1863, the same year that Speke and Grant were to emerge from the heart of Africa. It was the same year the Bakers were to begin their journey into the interior. In 1863 Egypt was prosperous, and because of the American Civil War, cotton prices were high. Egyptian cotton prices were five times higher than they had been in 1860. Also, the Suez Canal opened in 1869. Egypt owned 40 percent of the Canal stock, so the Canal tolls added to Egypt's financial well-being.

Slavery had become a major political issue. Both Europe and America put pressure on Egypt to end Arab slave trading. The Khedive Ismail was politically clever. He wanted to give Europe (especially England) the *impression* that he was doing something to end slavery. In 1869 he asked Sir Samuel and Lady Baker for their help. The Bakers were now fully recovered from their difficult trip to Lake Albert and back and had maintained an interest in African affairs. Ismail knew he could use them.

Ismail asked Sir Samuel to take charge of a military expedition. Its goal was to annex the upper Nile (the Sudan) to Egypt. Ismail convinced Baker that such a move would go far to end slave trading in that region.

Baker believed Ismail. Perhaps Baker was a little naive. It was well known, after all, that Ismail owned a great many slaves himself. Nonetheless, Baker accepted Ismail's proposal and found himself the prime agent of Ismail's plans to make the upper Nile a colony of Egypt.

By 1871 the Bakers were in Gondokoro. On May 20 they officially annexed the country surrounding Gondokoro to Egypt and called it Equatoria. The Bakers then went on to Bunyoro, where they promptly annexed that region to Egypt. But native forces chased them out, and they eventually retreated to Fatiko and built a fort there. The Bakers returned to Cairo in August 1873 when their five-year commission ran out. They were convinced they had eliminated slave trading from the Nile valley. In fact, slave trading was stronger than ever in the Sudan. It was just not quite as obvious.

The Khedive Ismail spent much of Egypt's cotton wealth on his private projects. He spent so much that he put Egypt into deep debt. He eventually had to sell Egypt's shares in the Suez Canal to keep his country from going bankrupt. (Ironically, England bought the shares.) But nothing would stop Ismail from conquering the upper Nile.

After the Bakers left Africa in 1873, Ismail had to find someone else to take charge in Equatoria. His final choice was Colonel Charles George Gordon of the British Royal Engineers. Gordon had served with great bravery in the Crimean War and in China. On January 28, 1874, Gordon set off for Egypt. He liked the Khedive Ismail right away and fully approved Ismail's plan to expand Egypt all the way to Lake Victoria. Gordon agreed to set up military outposts along the Nile from Gondokoro to Lake Victoria. He also hoped to launch steamers on Lakes Victoria and Albert, and was instructed to abolish slave trade along the route. Ismail felt obliged, again, to add this instruction to appease the English.

So began Gordon's work in Africa. He was to continue in Africa, off and on, for the next eleven years. Gordon first moved his headquarters from Gondokoro to Lado. Then he proceeded up the river, mapping it as he went. He set up military outposts along the way to secure the river. Two steamers, the *Nyanza* and the *Khedive*, were carried up the Nile in pieces and put together again on Lake Albert. After two and a half years on the Nile, Gordon had made it safe for travel from Gondokoro to Lake Albert. Slave trading had been abolished along the way. Gordon's dozen forts along the Nile were remarkable and several became settled townships. Most amazing of all, Gordon managed to make friends with all the local tribes along the way.

Despite his success, Gordon resigned his position at the end of 1876. The slave trade he so wanted to abolish was too widespread. It did not involve simply the Nile valley, and Gordon felt he did not have enough power to bring it to an end. But he returned to Egypt in February 1877 when the Khedive made him an offer he could not refuse. Ismail made Gordon the governor of all the Sudan. Now Gordon had the power he wanted. And Ismail needed Gordon. Egypt was terribly in debt, and Ismail needed a strong governor in the Sudan to make sure *all* the wealth of the Sudan came back to Cairo. Ismail was even willing to sacrifice slave trading if necessary.

Gordon entered Khartoum from the east on May 4, 1877, after traveling across land by camel through Abyssinia. Once in Khartoum he immediately began to write new laws and decrees. He was determined to "clean up" the Sudan. In his greatest personal triumph, he managed to bring an end to slave trading in the western Sudan through a brilliant, guerilla-like military operation.

But again, despite his success, Gordon was becoming uneasy. The Khedive Ismail had bankrupted Egypt. He had transferred all his private debts to the state. He increased taxes again and again, and the Egyptian national debt soared from £3,000,000 to £100,000,000. Under pressure from his European creditors, he was finally "deposed." He left Egypt on his yacht *Mahrousa* with about £3,000,000, and his eldest son, Tewfik, became the head of state. In July 1879 Gordon himself felt it was time to leave. He was to return one last time.

In the fall of 1881 the Khedive Tewfik was deposed. A group of Egyptian army officers under Ahmed Arabi led the bloodless coup. By May 1882 Arabi had become the virtual dictator of Egypt. Arabi's rule began a period of anti-European, anti-Christian feeling in Egypt and the Sudan. By June 1882 some fourteen thousand Europeans had left Cairo. Rioting broke out in Alexandria, and the British consul, Sir Charles Cookson, was badly hurt. A peaceful settlement seemed out of reach. The British public pressed more and more for war, and the British navy finally attacked Alexandria on July 11. But the decisive battle was at Tel-el-Kebir on September 13. The British won this skirmish easily, and from then until 1953 the British remained firmly in Egypt.

As soon as Gordon left the Sudan, the situation there began to worsen. The Egyptians were hated throughout the Sudan, as were the British. To the Sudanese, both were colonial powers depriving the Sudan of home rule. The Sudanese wanted all foreign influence out of their land.

The time was ripe for a revolutionary leader to appear; inevitably one did. He was Mohammed Ahmed Ibn el-Sayyid Abdullah. He called himself a Mahdi, or religious leader. He was a warrior-priest, determined to free the Sudan from the corrupt Egyptians and return his people to what he believed to be the "true" faith. The Mahdi's success was phenomenal. By 1883 all of Kordofan (the western Sudan) was in the Mahdi's hands. Egypt was determined to regain control over the region. The British would have nothing to do with this newest war; they felt it was a local matter that should be settled locally. But the British-backed government in Cairo put together an army to invade the Sudan. They found a British mercenary to command it: Colonel William Hicks.

Hicks's army of ten thousand made its way down the Nile, then across the desert toward El Obeid. On November 5, 1883, the Mahdi's force of fifty thousand descended on Hicks's men. Of the original ten thousand, only three hundred survived.

After the disaster at El Obeid, England put increasing pressure on Egypt to pull out of the Sudan. But Khartoum could not simply be abandoned. There had to be an orderly and peaceful withdrawal of the Egyptian garrison there. Many in England, including Sir Samuel Baker, felt the Mahdi should be defeated. Baker proposed sending in a British or Indian force under Gordon's command, but the British government, under the leadership of Prime Minister Gladstone, preferred the idea of orderly withdrawal. Gladstone did not want to involve England in local Sudanese affairs any more than was necessary. The public demanded that Gordon be sent to conduct the withdrawal. Gladstone was reluctant to send Gordon because Gordon clearly wanted war with the Mahdi. Finally it was decided: Gordon would be sent to Khartoum—as an *observer* only. He was to be given no troops.

On February 18, 1884, Gordon arrived in Khartoum for the last time. The people of the city welcomed him. Soon it became apparent in London that Gordon did not intend to evacuate the Khartoum garrison. He wrote: "If Egypt is to be kept quiet, the Mahdi must be smashed up." He then asked for £100,000 and two hundred Indian troops. "It would be comparatively easy to destroy the Mahdi," he concluded.

But Gordon was mistaken about the Mahdi and his power. He never received a reply to his request for troops and money, and on March 13, tribes north of Khartoum rose for the Mahdi. They cut the telegraph lines and blocked all Egyptian traffic on the Nile. Khartoum was now under siege. Little news came out of the Sudan for the next ten months.

The Mahdi knew he simply had to wait. Soon Khartoum would be starving and victory would be easy. Back in England public opinion ran high for the rescue of Gordon, who was immensely popular. Still, the true danger of his situation was not fully understood. The British consistently underestimated the Mahdi's power. So it was not until September 9, 1884—almost seven months later—that the British arrived in Cairo with troops, under the direction of Lord Wolseley.

But help for Gordon came too late. In the early morning of January 26, 1885, some fifty thousand of the Mahdi's supporters invaded Khartoum. They killed whomever they found—men, women, children. No one was spared.

Gordon was awakened by the fighting. From the roof of the Palace he could see the Arabs pressing toward him. He shot at them with a machine gun to no avail. When he saw that all was lost, he changed into his dress uniform and waited. The invaders found him at the head of the stairs. He was speared to death before he had a chance to fire his revolver.

The head was cut off Gordon's body and taken to the Mahdi. The body remained in the courtyard at the Palace where every passing Arab stuck his spear into it.

When Wolseley heard of Gordon's death and Khartoum's fall, he wanted to prepare for all-out war. But the government in London refused, and Wolseley's troops were forced to return to Cairo. For a while, at least, the Sudan was to be left to the Mahdists.

Only five months after Gordon's death, the Mahdi died at Omdurman. His successor, the Khalifa Abdullah, made sure the cult of the Mahdi lived on after the Mahdi's death. He was considered by many as equal to Mohammed, the founder of Islam. A great tomb was built at Omdurman. Soon there were pilgrimages to the Mahdi's tomb like the pilgrimages to Mohammed's birthplace in Mecca.

In England a similar, if less religious, cult formed around Gordon. Clearly, the public wanted revenge for his death. The Mahdist state under the Khalifa was seen as totally evil and the British public felt a real hatred for the Khalifa and his people. But the British were far from idle while they waited for their revenge.

Through a series of agreements and power plays, Britain gained control of Kenya. The British East Africa Company had bases throughout what was to become Uganda. The head of the Company in Africa, F. D. Lugard, convinced the British public and the Queen that Uganda needed British protection. In April 1894 Uganda officially became a British protectorate. Now the British had Egypt at the mouth of the Nile and Uganda at its source. All that remained to give them complete control of the Nile was the Sudan.

The Sudanese had been greatly weakened by smallpox and syphilis. Also, the Khalifa had exterminated masses of his own people who had opposed him. Then, in 1889, there was a plague of locusts which destroyed crops. Famine followed. The Sudan was becoming ever weaker.

By 1896 the British were prepared to strike. It was long past time to avenge Gordon's death. But perhaps even more important at the time, Britain was afraid France would take the Sudan if Britain did not. With the Sudan, Britain would have control of the entire Nile valley, then east all the way to the Indian Ocean.

The job of conquering the Sudan fell to General Horatio Herbert Kitchener. Ten thousand Egyptian and British troops

*On January 26, 1885,
after ten long months
of siege, the Mahdi's forces
overran Khartoum and
Colonel Gordon was killed.*

with British officers began to assemble under Kitchener's direction in 1896. The British navy commandeered all the pleasure steamers that were making sightseeing runs on the lower Nile, and over the next two years Kitchener's force made its way carefully up the Nile. The Khalifa watched and waited in the depths of the Sudan. Then, in April 1898, he came to meet the British and Egyptian force at Atbara. The Khalifa's most aggressive general, the Emir Mahmoud, was in charge of the Mahdist forces. Kitchener and his troops attacked the Mahdist barricades while a military band played. Before long the battle was over. Some two thousand of the Mahdist forces lay dead, and their general was captured and paraded in chains through the nearby town of Berber.

Kitchener's next stop was Omdurman, which he reached by September 1, 1898. By then he had a force of twenty thousand, including gunboats and one hundred large pieces of artillery. The Khalifa's force of fifty thousand was waiting. Their guns were obsolete, and many had only spears as weapons. It was like a repeat of Napoleon's encounters with the Turks. At dawn on September 2, the Khalifa's force attacked and rushed straight into the British artillery fire.

The Khalifa's forces never even reached the British and Egyptian front lines. Their headlong assault was desperate, foolhardy, and brave. By noon, ten thousand of the Mahdists were dead and thousands more were injured. The survivors made a hasty retreat toward Omdurman. Kitchener's casualties were four hundred.

Kitchener marched into Omdurman with little opposition. He was told the Khalifa had escaped toward El Obeid. British cavalry went after the Khalifa, but several days later turned back empty-handed. Kitchener set up his headquarters in the mosque at Omdurman.

But matters in the Sudan were not quite settled. The French had sent a small military division across Africa from the west. These troops now positioned themselves across the Nile at Fashoda. Kitchener was under orders to rout them. The French would be allowed no part of the Sudan. Kitchener met with the French commander, Captain Marchand, and stated the English position. Both men agreed to let their governments decide. For a while it seemed that Britain and France might go to war in Europe over possession of the Sudan, but finally France surrendered Fashoda to England. A European war was avoided, for the time being.

One final matter required attention. The Khalifa was still at large. He and his followers were located in October 1899. Kitchener sent a detachment to capture or kill the Khalifa; he was determined to wipe out all the Mahdists. The British caught up with the Khalifa on November 23. A brief battle took place at dawn. The Khalifa and other Mahdist leaders were killed, and some twenty-nine others were captured. Kitchener could finally say, in his official report, "Mahdism is now a thing of the past."

Now, too, the Nile belonged to England, from its source in Uganda to its mouth. On paper the Egyptians were joint rulers with England of most of the Nile valley. But in fact, it was England that ruled. For the first time in history, the entire length of the Nile was open and united, from Lake Victoria to the Mediterranean.

CHAPTER SEVEN

THE NILE IN THE TWENTIETH CENTURY

Under the British the Nile would be exploited as never before. By 1902 the first Aswan dam had been built. Its level was raised twice—in 1912 and 1933. By 1933 the Aswan reservoir could hold five times more water than it could in 1902. But still this original Aswan Dam could only catch the end of the yearly Nile flood. Engineers did not want to make the dam too large because the Nile flood carries a lot of sediment with it. It was feared that a large reservoir would fill up with this sediment very quickly.

Instead, a number of small dams were built downstream from the Aswan Dam. These small dams would trap some of the water let through the big dam during the flood. This water could then be used for local irrigation. Besides the Delta dams built in the nineteenth century by Muhammed Ali, new ones were put up at Assiut (1902), Zifta (1903), Isna (1909), Nag Hammadi (1930), and Edfina (1951).

The British also went ahead with construction of a dam in the Sudan—the Sennar Dam on the Blue Nile (1926). It provided irri-

Irrigated cotton fields and date orchards
in the Nile Delta

gation water for a huge cotton-growing region called the Gezira Cotton Scheme.

All of the British ideas for water storage were part of a grand plan called the Century Storage Scheme. This scheme was to make the Nile completely controllable by storing up several years of floods in various reservoirs. The water would be released as needed. The Century Storage Scheme involved some twenty different projects in nine African nations. The heart of the project was a dam at Lake Victoria. This lake was to be used as a major reservoir. It would store water all year long, not just at time of flood. This dam was never built, but a smaller dam to generate electricity was built between 1948 and 1954. It is the Owen Falls Dam and supplies 150 megawatts of power to Ugandan industry every year.

The Century Storage Scheme also proposed a canal around the Sudd, the great swamp in the Sudan through which the Nile runs. Channeling the Nile around the swamp would end the problem of evaporation. Unfortunately, it would also totally alter the environment of the area. It would cause the displacement of a large number of people who lived there. The idea of this canal was finally abandoned as the Sudan moved toward independence in 1955.

The Jebel Auliya Dam just south of Khartoum was not part of the Century Storage Scheme. It was built in 1937 to provide more summer water for Egypt. The Sennar Dam on the Blue Nile had taken some of that water away, making the Jebel Auliya Dam necessary.

There was also to be a dam on Lake Tana at the source of the Blue Nile. Like the intended dam on Lake Victoria, it would turn Lake Tana into a reservoir that could hold more than one year's flood, but nothing ever came of this plan. Lake Tana lies in Ethiopia, and negotiations have never been easy between Christian Ethiopia and its Moslem neighbors.

Only one other dam was built on the Blue Nile, and that was in 1966. It is the Roseires Dam and it supplies water to the

Managil extension of the Gezira Cotton Scheme. This dam has silted up very rapidly. Between 1966 and 1975 the reservoir went from a depth of 167 feet (50 m) to a depth of 56 feet (17 m).

All interest in the Century Storage Scheme came to a sudden halt in 1952. Egypt had been given its "independence" from Britain in 1923, but British troops were still in Egypt, and British influence was strong. The Egyptian monarchy could not have existed without British backing. On July 23, 1952, a group of Egyptian army officers led a nationalist revolt and took power. The Egyptian king abdicated shortly thereafter. The Egyptian people welcomed the new regime, which demanded that Britain leave Egypt altogether, including the Suez Canal. The British evacuated in June 1953. Under the new regime General Naguib was the first president, but not for long. Colonel Gamal Abdel Nasser ousted him in a power struggle and became president himself in 1956.

The new regime was full of vision and hope and wanted to make a grand gesture to the Egyptian people and the world. The government wanted everyone to know that things would be different in the new era. It soon became clear that the grand gesture would be the Aswan High Dam. Within two months of the July Revolution, the Revolutionary Command Council was considering the project.

The High Dam would provide the yearly water storage Egypt needed. It would provide electricity for industry, and it would stand as a symbol to the world of Egypt's determination to modernize.

Original funding for the project was to come from Western sources. But the United States and Great Britain began to mistrust Nasser. Nasser seemed openly hostile to the West. When Nasser nationalized the Suez Canal, relations with the West got worse. Increasingly, Nasser turned toward the Soviet Union for aid. At first the aid was mostly military, but more and more the Soviets were considered for funding the High Dam. The Western powers did not think the Soviets would come through, and they

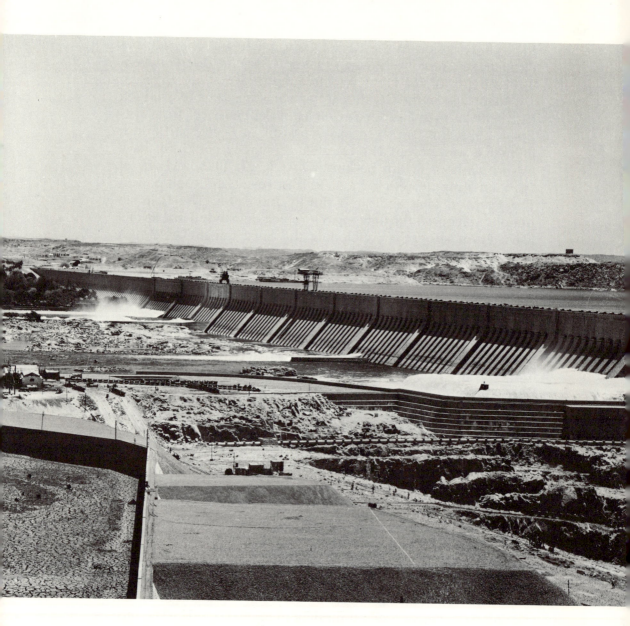

The Aswan High Dam

hoped Nasser would be forced to depend on Western aid. But on October 23, 1958, the Soviet leader Nikita Khrushchev told the Egyptians that his country would give them about $100 million in loan guarantees toward construction of the High Dam.

From then on the High Dam was a joint Egyptian-Soviet venture. For the Egyptians it became a symbol of resistance to Western demands. For the Soviets it became a showplace of Soviet technology and a focus of Soviet influence in the Middle East. Further agreements with the Soviets were reached. Arrangements with the Sudanese government were also completed and work on the High Dam began on January 9, 1960.

By May 1964 a rock-filled coffer dam was finished. This structure diverted the Nile's waters and allowed construction of the main dam. The Aswan High Dam was opened on January 15, 1971. Nasser did not live to see it completed. His successor, Anwar el-Sadat, was at the opening with Nikolai Podgorny, President of the USSR. Ironically, Sadat's government became quickly anti-Soviet. By 1976 all Soviet influence was gone from Egypt.

The Aswan High Dam is an incredible engineering feat. It is over 2¼ miles (3.6 km) long and 360 feet (108 m) high. It is 3,200 feet (960 m) thick at the base and 130 feet (39 m) thick at the top. It can produce 10 billion kilowatt-hours of electricity every year. The reservoir behind the dam, called Lake Nasser, is 310 miles (496 km) long and 6 to 18 miles (9.6 to 29 km) wide. At the highest levels it is 600 feet (180 m) deep.

The High Dam has brought both good and bad with it. On the good side, additional land is being reclaimed from the desert as more irrigation water becomes available. Upper Egypt now receives year-round irrigation for the first time. Rice acreage has expanded beyond all expectation. Also, Egypt no longer faces danger from high floods, and navigation on the river has improved by eliminating the annual flood. The Sudan has benefited, too. It can now keep more of its own water for its own use, which has improved relations between the Sudan and Egypt.

But there have been problems with the High Dam. Almost half the water flowing into the High Dam is lost in evaporation and seepage. This loss is much higher than was at first thought. Also, the soil downstream from the dam is not as fertile as it once was. The annual flood used to bring silt with it and the silt made the land fertile. But the irrigation water from the dam has no silt, so now artificial fertilizers have to be used.

In many areas the land is irrigated too much. The result is waterlogging. Without proper drainage, water evaporates from the surface rather than seeping through. This evaporation leaves salts behind which make the land unusable. Up to 90 percent of cultivated Egyptian land is waterlogged. Some 35 percent has problems with too great a salt content.

The High Dam has also increased coastal erosion. The Delta is actually shrinking. It was already shrinking before the High Dam was built, but the High Dam has increased the speed of the shrinking as more and more silt stays behind the dam. The silt which once built the Delta no longer makes its way to the sea.

The High Dam has never provided as much electricity as promised. Its total possible output is 10 billion kilowatt-hours per year. In fact it has never generated more than 7 billion kilowatt-hours per year. For technical reasons, the High Dam will probably never produce electricity to full capacity.

But perhaps the saddest result of the High Dam's construction was the flooding of Nubia. The banks of the Nile south of Aswan were lined with many temples and tombs of the ancient Egyptians. A number of these monuments are lost forever under the waters of Lake Nasser. But a massive international effort was made to save some of the monuments. In all, fourteen were preserved. Ten are still in Egypt, moved to higher ground near the Nile, and four smaller ones were given to the countries that helped most in the massive moving projects. One of these temples, the Temple of Dendur, is now in the Metropolitan Museum of Art in New York City. It was originally situated 50 miles (80 km) south of Aswan.

The Temple of Abu Simbel was moved at a cost of millions of dollars to save it from floodwaters of the Aswan Dam project.

The largest and most difficult move was of the temple complex called Abu Simbel. Many plans were proposed to save it. One group even wanted to surround it with glass. They believed the complex could then be left underwater, which would obviously make viewing it difficult. Finally Abu Simbel was moved to higher ground against a cliff, to look just like it did originally.

The temple and its giant statues had been carved out of the side of a mountain. In order to move Abu Simbel, it first had to be separated from the mountain. Then it was cut into movable pieces. Slowly the pieces were moved to higher ground and put back together. The project took nine years. It cost millions of dollars, but a priceless monument was saved. And visitors to Egypt are still helping to pay for the move. The price of every Egyptian visa goes to pay for the cost of moving Abu Simbel.

Despite its problems, the Aswan High Dam has brought Egypt firmly into the modern age. It has helped make Egypt the most powerful Moslem nation in the Middle East. It stands like the ancient monuments on the Nile, as a symbol of power and determination. It is the latest and most successful attempt to control the river that has given Egypt life for seven thousand years—the mighty Nile.

INDEX